# Shoes in Indian Culture

## The Bata Shoe Museum, Toronto
### A BOOK OF POSTCARDS

*Pomegranate*

SAN FRANCISCO

Pomegranate Communications, Inc.
Box 6099, Rohnert Park, CA 94927
800-227-1428
www.pomegranate.com

Pomegranate Europe Ltd.
Fullbridge House, Fullbridge
Maldon, Essex CM9 4LE, England

ISBN 0-7649-2134-7
Pomegranate Catalog No. AA181

Pomegranate publishes books of
postcards on a wide range of subjects.
Please contact the publisher for more information.

Cover designed by Patrice Morris
Printed in China
11 10 09 08 07 06 05 04 03 02   10 9 8 7 6 5 4 3 2 1

To facilitate detachment of the postcards from this book, fold each card along its perforation line before tearing.

**A**s Indian culture and religion perceive it, the foot is a venerable and highly significant appendage. The young worship not at their elders' feet: they worship the feet themselves. The devout adore the feet of holy men and religious images. And lovers find that one another's feet hold a powerful romantic and erotic charge.

As recently as fifty years ago, India was described as a "barefoot country." Ascetic Hindus, Jains, and Buddhists considered shoes a worldly indulgence. Sandals were primarily confined to the feet of mendicant monks, and shoes to the feet of those who lived in harsh country; only the very wealthy wore the gorgeously silver- and gold-embroidered slippers that Westerners imagine when they think of traditional Indian clothing.

Still, shoes, sandals, slippers, and boots were worn. Perhaps because of their rarity and value, a number of them have survived, in fine condition—some for hundreds and even thousands of years. (The earliest known Indian sandal, excavated in western Bengal, has been dated to approximately 200 B.C., and the *Rig Veda,* approximately 6,000 years old, makes mention of foot and ankle ornaments.)

The images in this book of postcards were selected from about 130 photographs that appeared in *Feet & Footwear in Indian Culture* (The Bata Shoe Museum Foundation/Mapin Publishing Pvt. Ltd., 2000), a book written by Jutta Jain-Neubauer and sponsored by The Bata Shoe Museum of Toronto—the largest shoe collection in the world. The photographs reproduced here offer a fascinating (and aesthetically rewarding) peek at the footwear of a vast, colorful, ancient, and bewilderingly diverse accumulation of cultures, from ancient times to the late twentieth century. ✺

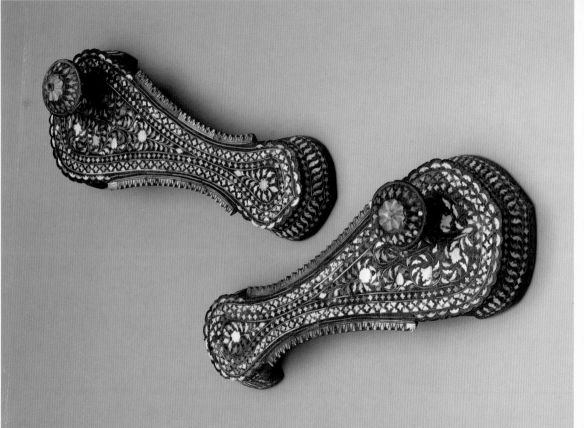

# **Shoes** in Indian Culture

Wooden *padukas* with ivory inlay in abstract and floral motifs
India
Collection of The Bata Shoe Museum, Toronto
Photograph by John Bigelow Taylor

BOX 6099  ROHNERT PARK  CA 94927

Pomegranate

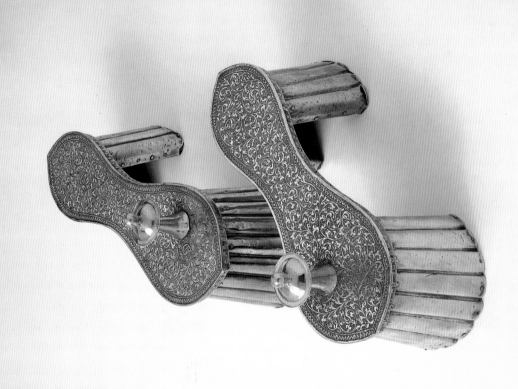

# **Shoes** in Indian Culture

Ceremonial silver *padukas* with ornamental gold-covered toe knobs
Jaipur, India, eighteenth century
Collection of The Bata Shoe Museum, Toronto
Photograph by John Bigelow Taylor

BOX 6099     ROHNERT PARK     CA 94927

Pomegranate

# **Shoes** in Indian Culture

Fish-shaped wooden *padukas* with inlaid brass wire,
featuring stylized scales and tail fins
South Bengal, India
Collection of The Bata Shoe Museum, Toronto
Photograph by John Bigelow Taylor

BOX 6099   ROHNERT PARK   CA 94927

Pomegranate

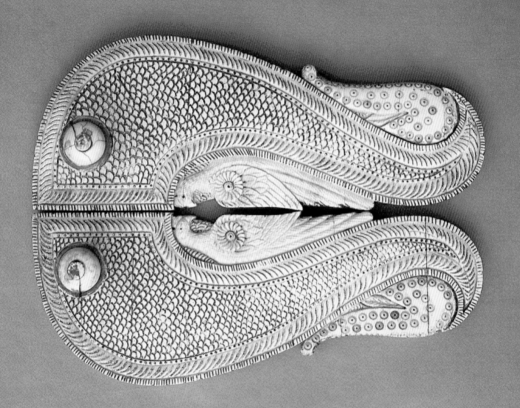

# Shoes in Indian Culture

Ivory *padukas* carved with fish scale pattern and stylized birds
India
Collection of Sanskriti Museum of Everyday Art, New Delhi

BOX 6099    ROHNERT PARK    CA 94927

*Pomegranate*

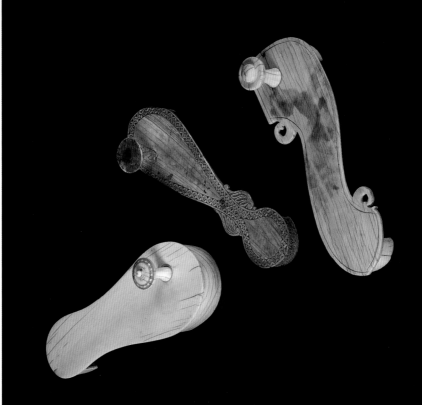

# **Shoes** in Indian Culture

*Padukas* made of precious ivory were worn by Indian holy men and royalty.
India
Collection of The Bata Shoe Museum, Toronto
Photograph by John Bigelow Taylor

BOX 6099    ROHNERT PARK    CA 94927

Pomegranate

# Shoes in Indian Culture

Foot-shaped metal *padukas*
Jaipur, India, late eighteenth century
Collection of The Bata Shoe Museum, Toronto
Photograph by John Bigelow Taylor

BOX 6099   ROHNERT PARK   CA 94927

Pomegranate

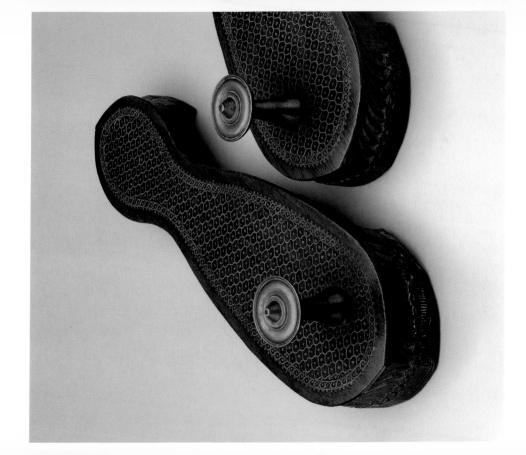

# Shoes in Indian Culture

Wooden *padukas* with inlaid brass wire decoration
India
Collection of The Bata Shoe Museum, Toronto
Photograph by John Bigelow Taylor

BOX 6099   ROHNERT PARK   CA 94927

Pomegranate

# **Shoes** in Indian Culture

*Mojaris* embroidered with gold thread and embellished with gems;
worn by the Nizam of Hyderabad
Hyderabad, Andhra Pradesh, India, 1790–1820
Collection of The Bata Shoe Museum, Toronto
Photograph by John Bigelow Taylor

BOX 6099    ROHNERT PARK    CA 94927

*Pomegranate*

# Shoes in Indian Culture

Two-horned shoe worn by Brahmins
Mumbai (city of Bombay), Maharashtra, India, c. 1879
Collection of The Bata Shoe Museum, Toronto
Photograph by John Bigelow Taylor

BOX 6099  ROHNERT PARK  CA 94927

Pomegranate

# Shoes in Indian Culture

Embroidered velvet *juttis* for court wear
Sri Lanka, 1875–1887
Collection of The Bata Shoe Museum, Toronto
Photograph by Peter Patterson

BOX 6099   ROHNERT PARK   CA 94927

Pomegranate

# Shoes in Indian Culture

Silver slippers with Ganga Jamuna design and red velvet lining
North India, twentieth century
Collection of The Bata Shoe Museum, Toronto
Photograph by John Bigelow Taylor

BOX 6099    ROHNERT PARK    CA 94927

Pomegranate

# Shoes in Indian Culture

Ceremonial silver-mesh shoes, possibly for a wedding or dowry gift
North India, nineteenth century
Collection of The Bata Shoe Museum, Toronto
Photograph by John Bigelow Taylor

BOX 6099   ROHNERT PARK   CA 94927

Pomegranate

# Shoes in Indian Culture

Repoussé silver shoes with incised designs, probably
a wedding or dowry gift
Patiala, Punjab, India, c. 1830
Collection of The Bata Shoe Museum, Toronto
Photograph by Peter Patterson

BOX 6099   ROHNERT PARK   CA 94927

Pomegranate

# **Shoes** in Indian Culture

Three men's *mojaris,* or *khussas,* with upturned toes
and gold and silver embroidery
India
Collection of The Bata Shoe Museum, Toronto
Photograph by John Bigelow Taylor

BOX 6099    ROHNERT PARK    CA 94927

Pomegranate

# Shoes in Indian Culture

Women's dress *juttis* embroidered with delicate designs
India, mid-twentieth century
Collection of The Bata Shoe Museum, Toronto
Photograph by John Bigelow Taylor

Pomegranate    BOX 6099    ROHNERT PARK    CA 94927

# **Shoes** in Indian Culture

Gold-embroidered *mojaris,* called *khussas,* first became
popular during the Mughal period
India
Collection of The Bata Shoe Museum, Toronto
Photograph by Peter Patterson

BOX 6099   ROHNERT PARK   CA 94927

*Pomegranate*

# Shoes in Indian Culture

Gold-embroidered bridegroom's shoe and heeled woman's shoe
inspired by Western fashions
India, early twentieth century
Collection of The Bata Shoe Museum, Toronto
Photograph by Peter Patterson

BOX 6099   ROHNERT PARK   CA 94927

Pomegranate

# **Shoes** in Indian Culture

Kolhapuri buffalo leather *chappals* with toe rings
India
Collection of The Bata Shoe Museum, Toronto
Photograph by Peter Patterson

BOX 6099    ROHNERT PARK    CA 94927

*Pomegranate*

# Shoes in Indian Culture

(Left) Open-toed *kwati* sandal with gold embroidery
Punjab, India, twentieth century
(Right) Crossed-strap *peshawari* sandals embellished
with gold and textile embroidery
Punjab, India, nineteenth–twentieth century
Collection of The Bata Shoe Museum, Toronto
Photograph by John Bigelow Taylor

BOX 6099 ROHNERT PARK CA 94927

Pomegranate

# **Shoes** in Indian Culture

Wooden stilt sandals, decorated with carved designs
Swat Valley, Pakistan
Collection of The Bata Shoe Museum, Toronto
Photograph by Peter Patterson

BOX 6099   ROHNERT PARK   CA 94927

*Pomegranate*

# **Shoes** in Indian Culture

Crossed multistrapped sandal with a central toe strap (called a *nokh*)
and laced leather sock
Chamba, Himachal Pradesh, India, c. 1895
Collection of The Bata Shoe Museum, Toronto
Photograph by Peter Patterson

BOX 6099   ROHNERT PARK   CA 94927

Pomegranate

# Shoes in Indian Culture

*Juttis* embellished with chain stitch embroidery worked with a hook
Punjab region, India, twentieth century
Collection of The Bata Shoe Museum, Toronto
Photograph by Peter Patterson

BOX 6099   ROHNERT PARK   CA 94927

*Pomegranate*

# Shoes in Indian Culture

*Juttis* with keyhole-shaped soles, called *kannali*
Collection of The Bata Shoe Museum, Toronto
Photograph by Peter Patterson

BOX 6099   ROHNERT PARK   CA 94927

Pomegranate

# **Shoes** in Indian Culture

Heavy rural *juttis* made of buffalo and cow leather, worn
by farmers and herdsmen
Punjab region, India, nineteenth–twentieth century
Collection of The Bata Shoe Museum, Toronto
Photograph by Peter Patterson

BOX 6099   ROHNERT PARK   CA 94927

Pomegranate

# Shoes in Indian Culture

*Tauranwari juttis* are perfectly suited to a desert environment.
The thin backs make it easy to flick out trapped sand.
Central Sindh, Pakistan
Collection of The Bata Shoe Museum, Toronto
Photograph by John Bigelow Taylor

BOX 6099   ROHNERT PARK   CA 94927

Pomegranate

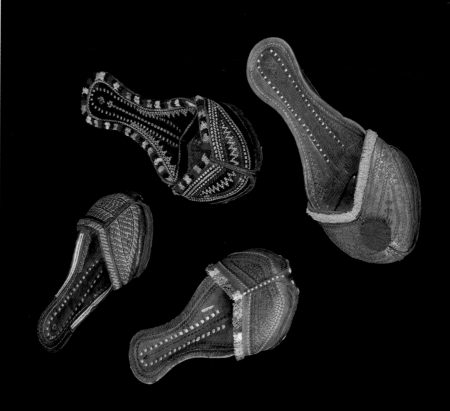

# **Shoes** in Indian Culture

*Juttis* decorated with interlaced leather strips, leather underlay,
and colorful embroidery
Gujarat, India, 1960–1985
Collection of The Bata Shoe Museum, Toronto
Photograph by John Bigelow Taylor

CA 94927

ROHNERT PARK

BOX 6099

*Pomegranate*

# **Shoes** in Indian Culture

Felted wool *jhaalaam* boots
Tibet, nineteenth century
Collection of The Bata Shoe Museum, Toronto
Photograph by Peter Patterson

Pomegranate

BOX 6099   ROHNERT PARK   CA 94927

# Shoes in Indian Culture

Indo-Tibetan boots. Toe shapes, decoration, and materials can indicate the wearer's regional affiliation and rank or status. The type of boot at right, called a *rhelzom,* could be worn by aristocrats, lamas, and gurus incarnate.
Collection of The Bata Shoe Museum, Toronto
Photograph by John Bigelow Taylor

BOX 6099    ROHNERT PARK    CA 94927

Pomegranate

# Shoes in Indian Culture

Plant fiber shoes insulate the wearer's feet from snow and mud.
Himalayan Valley
Collection of The Bata Shoe Museum, Toronto
Photograph by Peter Patterson

BOX 6099   ROHNERT PARK   CA 94927

*Pomegranate*